BSCS Science T.R.A.C.S.

An Elementary School Science Program

Investigating Plants

BSCS

KENDALL/HUNT PUBLISHING COMPANY
4050 Westmark Drive   Dubuque, Iowa 52002

BSCS Development Team

Nancy M. Landes, Project Director and Author, 1996-98

Gail C. Foster, Author

Colleen K. Steurer, Author

Vonna G. Pinney, Executive Assistant

Linda K. Ward, Senior Executive Assistant

Rodger W. Bybee, Principal Investigator, 1994-95

Harold Pratt, Project Director, 1994-96

Janet Chatlain Girard, Art Coordinator, 1994-96

BSCS Administrative Staff

Timothy H. Goldsmith, Chair, Board of Directors

Joseph D. McInerney, Director

Michael J. Dougherty, Assistant Director

Lynda B. Micikas, Assistant Director

Larry Satkowiak, Chief Financial Officer

Contributors/Consultants

Randall K. Backe, BSCS, Colorado Springs, Colorado

Judy L. Capra, Wheatridge, Colorado, free-lance writer

Michael J. Dougherty, BSCS, Colorado Springs, Colorado

B. Ellen Friedman, San Diego, California

Cathy Griswold, Lyons, Oregon

David A. Hanych, BSCS, Colorado Springs, Colorado

Jay Hackett, Greeley, Colorado

Debra A. Hannigan, Colorado Springs, Colorado, contributing author

Karen Hollweg, Washington, DC

Winston King, Bridgetown, Barbados

Paul Kuerbis, Colorado Springs, Colorado

Donald E. Maxwell, BSCS, Colorado Springs, Colorado

Marge Melle, Littleton, Colorado, free-lance writer

Lynda B. Micikas, BSCS, Colorado Springs, Colorado

Jean P. Milani, BSCS, Colorado Springs, Colorado

Renee Mitchell, Lakewood, Colorado, free-lance writer

Brenda S. McCreight, Colorado Springs, Colorado, contributing author

Mary McMillan, Boulder, Colorado

Carol D. Prekker, Broomfield, Colorado, contributing author

Patricia J. Smith, Tucson, Arizona, contributing author

Terry Spencer, Monterey, California, contributing author

Patti M. Thorn, Austin, Texas, contributing author

Bonnie Turnbull, Monument, Colorado, free-lance writer

Terri B. Weber, Colorado Springs, Colorado

Carol A. Nelson Woller, Boulder, Colorado, contributing author

Field-Test Teachers and Coordinators, Levels 1-3

Joanne Allen, Grade 3, Westport Elementary School, Westport, Maine

Helene Auger, Westport School District, Westport, Maine

Sheila Dallas, Grade 2, Bethany School, Cincinnati, Ohio

Library of Congress Catalog Number: 97-76767

ISBN 0-7872-2258-5

Pat Dobosenski, Grade 3, Pembroke Elementary School, Troy, Michigan

Nina Finkel, Grade 1, Whitter Elementary School, Chicago, Illinois

Mary Elizabeth France, Grade 2, Westport Elementary School, Westport, Maine

Carolyn Gardner, Grade 3, Calhan Elementary School, Calhan, Colorado

Shelly Gordon, Grade 2, Bingham Farms Elementary School, Birmingham, Michigan

Darlene Grunert, Birmingham Public Schools, Birmingham, Michigan

Terry Heinecke, Grade 1, Edgerton Elementary School, Kalispell, Montana

Katherine Hickey, Grade 1, Irving Primary School, Highland Park, New Jersey

Jan Himmelspach, Grade 1, Grayson Elementary School, Waterford, Michigan

Janet Smith-James, Grade 3, Bartle School, Highland Park, New Jersey

Elizabeth Lankes, Grade 3, Bethany School, Glendale, Ohio

Barbara O'Neal, Grade 1, Calhan Elementary School, Calhan, Colorado

Cheryl Pez, Grade 2, Bethany School, Cincinnati, Ohio

Rochelle Rubin, Waterford School District-IMC, Waterford, Michigan

Elizabeth A. Smith, Grade 3, Grayson Elementary School, Waterford, Michigan

Melanie W. Smith, Grade 2, Washington Elementary School, Raleigh, North Carolina

Catherine Snyder, Highland Park School District, Highland Park, New Jersey

Ingrid Snyder, Grade 1, Waterford Village School, Waterford, Michigan

Lee Ann Van Horn, Wake County Public School System, Raleigh, North Carolina

Kathy Wright, Calhan Elementary School, Calhan, Colorado

Reviewers, Levels 1-3

James P. Barufaldi, University of Texas, Austin, Texas

Larry W. Esposito, University of Colorado at Boulder, Boulder, Colorado

Brenda S. Evans, Department of Education, Raleigh, North Carolina

Randy Gray, National Weather Service, Pueblo, Colorado

Judith Johnson, University of Central Florida, Orlando, Florida

Eric Leonard, The Colorado College, Colorado Springs, Colorado

Brownie Linder, Northern Arizona University, Flagstaff, Arizona

Jerry Ludwig, Fox Lane High School, Bedford, New York

Mike Madsen, KKTV, Channel 11, Colorado Springs, Colorado

Kathleen Roth, Michigan State University, East Lansing, Michigan

Cherilynn A. Morrow, Space Science Institute, Boulder, Colorado

Barbara W. Saigo, Saiwood Biology Resources, Montgomery, Alabama

Gail Shroyer, Kansas State University, Manhattan, Kansas

Carol Snell, University of Central Florida, Orlando, Florida

Joseph Stepans, University of Wyoming, Laramie, Wyoming

Richard Storey, The Colorado College, Colorado Springs, Colorado

Joan Tephly, Marycrest University, Iowa City, Iowa

Jack Wheatley, North Carolina State University, Raleigh, North Carolina

CONTENTS

Investigating Plants

Introduction   **Doing Science**   1

LESSON 1   Let's Get Growing   19

LESSON 2   A Package for Plants   27

LESSON 3   Knowing They Are Growing   35

LESSON 4   Investigating Plants' Needs   45

LESSON 5   Plant Part Chart   55

LESSON 6   Needs and Structures   65

LESSON 7   Plant Patrol   75

LESSON 8   My Plant Book   85

INTRODUCTION

Doing Science

What Is Science?

science...

scientist...

Read these questions. Draw pictures to show
what you think.

1. What do people do when they do science?

2. What is a scientist like?

3. Can you be a scientist right now?

4. What would you be doing if you were doing science?

How Can You Do Science?

Wonder

Ask questions

Observe with your senses

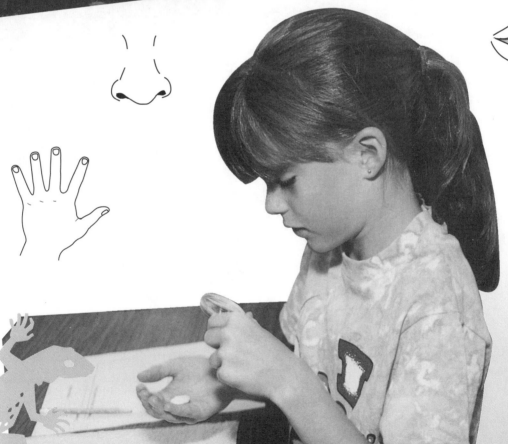

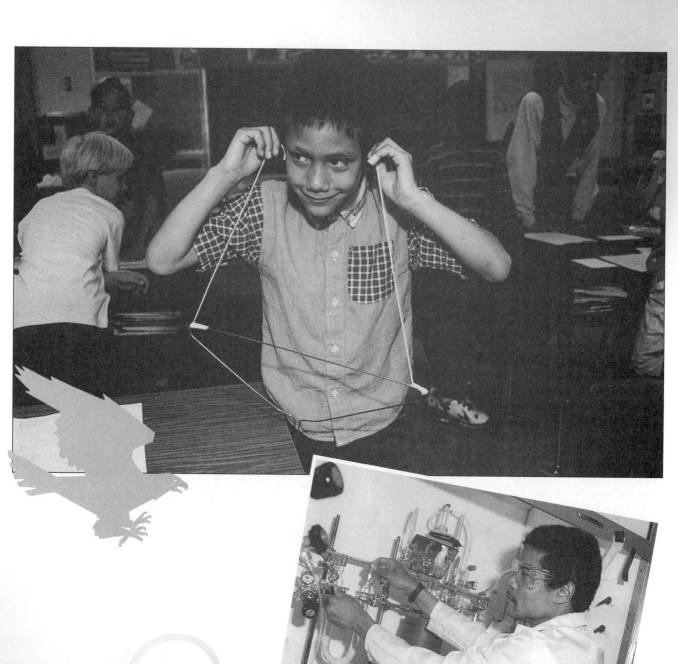

Investigate

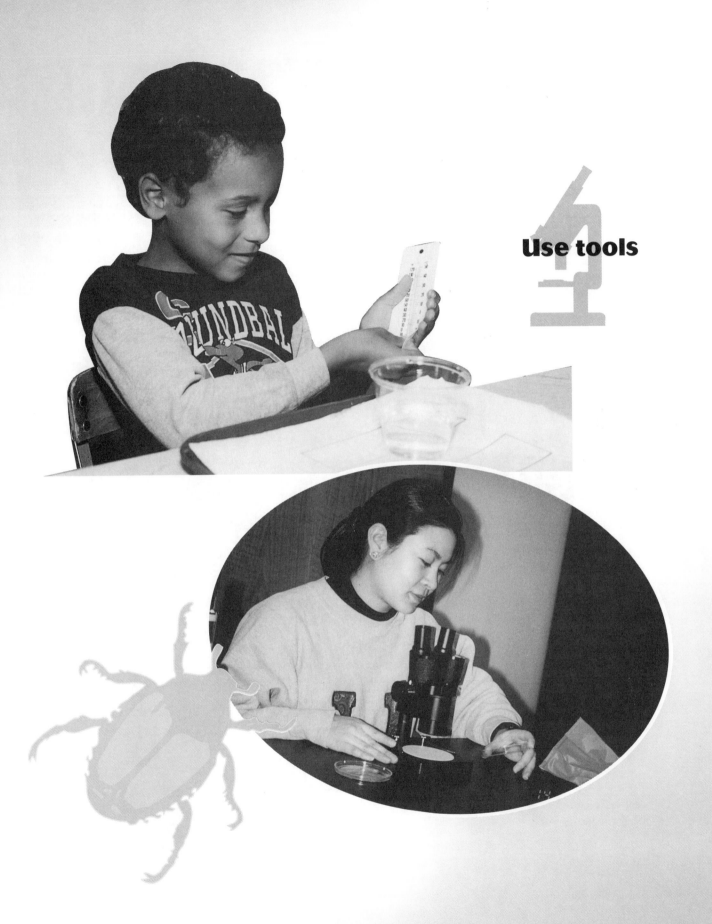

Use tools

Record by writing and drawing

Wonder and ask new questions

Working Together to Do Science

Move into your teams quickly and quietly.

Stay with your teams.

Speak softly.

Share and take turns.

Do your job.

Manager

Tracker

Messenger

Ask for help and give help.

What can you do if you need help?
What can you do to help your teammates?

The manager gets the supplies and returns them.

The tracker makes sure that the team follows the directions in order.

The messenger may ask another messenger for help.

The messenger may ask the teacher for help.

Doing Science with C.Q. and I.O.

Hi.
My name is C.Q.
I am <u>C</u>urious. I ask a lot of <u>Q</u>uestions. That is how I got my name. Doing science helps me learn about the things I am curious about. It can help you, too. You can answer a lot of your own questions by doing science.

My name is I.O.
I like to <u>I</u>nvestigate things. I <u>O</u>bserve carefully, too. That is how I got my name. C.Q. and I can help you investigate things that you are curious about.

Look for C.Q. and I.O. in your student guide. They will help you do science like a scientist does.

These pictures ![icon][icon] will help you remember when to record something. You can record things that happen at other times, too.

Invitation to Do Science

Are you curious about the world around you? If you are, then you are ready to do science. Remember to ask questions, investigate, and share your ideas. **You can find out a lot by doing science!**

Let's Get Growing

In the story, Jack and the Beanstalk, a plant grows from beans.

Do you think that plants can grow from beans?

Let's find out!

Making a Plastic Bag Greenhouse

Sometimes people grow plants in special buildings called greenhouses. Now you will make your own greenhouse to find out if plants can grow from beans.

Team Task
Make a plastic bag greenhouse for each teammate. Use it to find out if plants can grow from beans.

Team Skills

Speak softly.
Share and take turns.

Team Jobs

Manager   Tracker   Messenger

Team Supplies

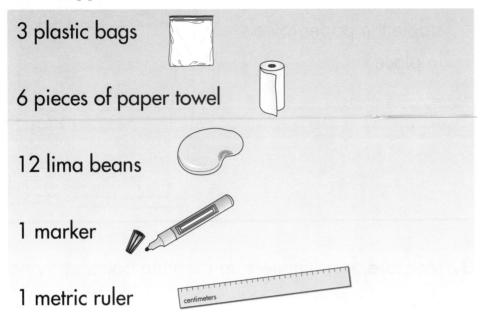

3 plastic bags

6 pieces of paper towel

12 lima beans

1 marker

1 metric ruler

Directions for Making a Plastic Bag Greenhouse

Help each teammate make a greenhouse by doing these things.

1. Lay 2 paper towels inside the bag like this.

2. Near the top of the bag, staple the paper towels in place.

3. Measure 5 centimeters up from the bottom on one side of the bag.

▶ Make a dot with the marker.

▶ Repeat on the other side.

4. Draw a line to connect the dots.

5. Staple along the line.

6. Drop the beans into the bag in front of the paper towel.

  ▶ Remember to leave space between the beans.

Now, you have each made a greenhouse.

Doing an Investigation

You wonder if plants can grow from beans. Scientists wonder about things, too.

An **investigation** is what scientists do to find out. They start with an idea or a question.

An investigation helps scientists find out about their idea or question. You will use your greenhouse in an investigation. What question will you investigate?

 On Your Own

Keeping Records

Scientists keep records so they can remember what has happened during an investigation.

Your Task
Draw a picture to make a record of what your beans look like today. Draw a picture that shows what you think the beans will look like if they grow.

Your Supplies

1 hand lens

1 copy of My Amazing
Beans Record Page

1 pencil

Directions for Keeping Records

1. Look closely at the beans in your greenhouse.

2. Draw on your record page what your beans look
like today.

3. Draw a picture of what you think will happen to the beans during the investigation.

4. Put your record pages in your science folder.

Checking Understanding

Do these things on your own.

1. On one side of your paper, draw a picture of what you did to answer the question, "Can plants grow from beans? "

2. On the back of your paper, write or draw one new idea you now have about seeds or growing plants.

A Package for Plants

Can you solve this riddle?
Share your ideas with your classmates.

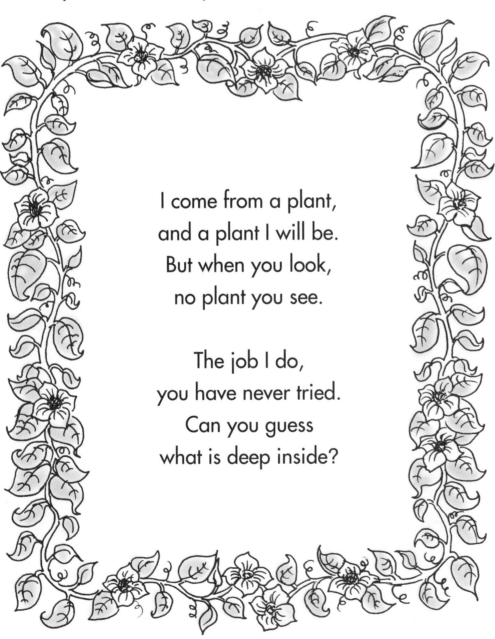

I come from a plant,
and a plant I will be.
But when you look,
no plant you see.

The job I do,
you have never tried.
Can you guess
what is deep inside?

What is Inside?

In the last lesson, you planted beans in greenhouses to find out if plants can grow from beans.
What do you think might be inside of a bean?

Team Task
Draw what you think is inside a bean. Share your pictures with your teammates.

Team Skill

Share and take turns.

Team Jobs

Manager

Tracker

Messenger

Team Supplies

3 Inside a Bean Record Pages

3 pencils

Directions for What is Inside?

1. Before you share your ideas as a team, do this by yourself. Use the top part of your own Inside a Bean Record Page. Draw a picture of what you think is inside a bean. This picture is your **prediction**.

2. When you are finished, share your drawings with your teammates.

   ▶ Take turns telling about your pictures.

   ▶ Tell why you think the inside of a bean looks like this.

Finding Out What is Inside a Bean

Your pictures show what you think is inside a bean. How could you find out?

Team Task
Open beans and observe the insides. Draw a picture of what you see.

Team Jobs

Manager   Tracker   Messenger

Team Skill

Share and take turns.

Team Supplies

3 hand lenses

soaked beans

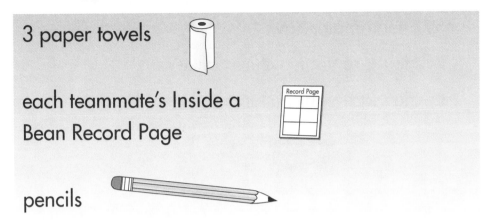

3 paper towels

each teammate's Inside a
Bean Record Page

pencils

Directions for Finding Out
What is Inside a Bean

1. Before you share your observations with your
   teammates, do these things by yourself.

   ▶ Peel the bean and pull the halves apart.

   ▶ Observe what is inside the bean.

   ▶ On the bottom part of your own Inside
     a Bean Record Page, draw what you see
     inside a bean.

2. Take turns telling your teammates about your
   picture.

Be very careful!

Remember to take turns.

3. Compare what you saw inside a bean to what your teammates saw.

▶ How are your pictures alike?

▶ How are your pictures different?

4. Compare the pictures on the bottom of your paper to the pictures on the top of your paper.

▶ Share how the pictures are alike.

▶ Share how the pictures are different.

5. Put your record pages in your science folder.

Sharing
IDEAS

You shared your pictures and observations with your teammates. Now, share your new ideas with your classmates.

Talk about these questions with the class.

1. What did you see that makes you think plants can grow from beans?

2. Did observing the insides of a bean change your mind about plants growing from beans? Why or why not?

3. What did you do to investigate the inside of a bean?

Checking Understanding

1. On your own, write about this question on your record page.

What is one new idea you have about beans?

2. With your teammates, do these things.

▶ Cut out the Investigation Cards.

▶ Talk about the steps you took to investigate the insides of beans.

▶ Put the Investigation Cards in order so they show the same steps that you took to investigate the insides of beans.

▶ Glue the cards to the Bean Investigation Record Page.

▶ Write your names on the back of the Bean Investigation Record Page.

▶ Post your Bean Investigation Record Page on the wall.

How Could You Find Out

What would you like to know about other packages for plants? You might wonder about questions like these. You can ask questions of your own, too.

- Is a sunflower seed like a bean?
- What is on the inside of other seeds?
- Do plants grow from different kinds of seeds?

Knowing They Are Growing

You planted beans in a plastic bag greenhouse to find out if plants can grow from beans.

You said the beans would need water to grow, so you added water to the beans in your greenhouse.

Are new plants growing from your beans?
How do you know?

On Your Own

Are They Growing?

Your Task
Record any changes you observe in the beans in your greenhouse.

Your Supplies

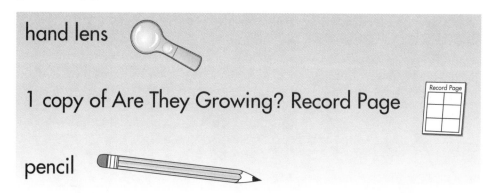

hand lens

1 copy of Are They Growing? Record Page

pencil

Directions for Are They Growing?

1. Observe the beans in your greenhouse.

2. On your record page, draw a picture of what your beans look like today.

3. Answer the question, "Can plants grow from beans? " Use your observations to tell why you think so.

4. Keep your record page so you can compare your observations to your classmates' observations.

Sharing and Comparing

By sharing your answers and comparing your observations, you can find out how your teammates answered the question and why they think so. Use your record pages to help you.

Share and compare your team's observations with your classmates' observations.

As a class, answer the question, "Can plants grow from beans? " Tell why you think so.

Which Plants Have Grown the Most?

How can you tell which plants have grown the most?

Measure the plants in all teammates' greenhouses. Show your **data** on graphs.

Team Skill

Ask for help and give help.

Team Jobs

Manager   Tracker   Messenger

Team Supplies

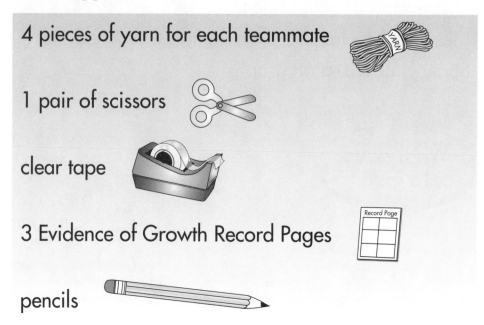

4 pieces of yarn for each teammate

1 pair of scissors

clear tape

3 Evidence of Growth Record Pages

pencils

Directions for Which Plants Have Grown The Most?

All teammates will help each other do these things.

1. Hold one end of the yarn even with the bottom of the bean. Lay the yarn along the stem of the plant.

Do not take the plants out of the greenhouses.

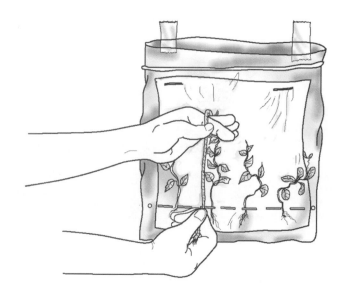

2. Cut the yarn even with the top of the plant.

3. Tape this piece of yarn on the first line of the
Evidence of Growth Record Page like this.

4. Repeat Steps 1 and 2 for the other plants in this
teammate's greenhouse.

5. Measure the plants and tape the yarn for the plants in the other teammates' greenhouses.

6. Compare your Evidence of Growth Record Page with your teammates' record pages.

Who has the tallest plant?

Who has the shortest?

7. Put your record pages in your science folder when you are finished.

Measuring and Describing

You found out that plants could grow from beans by observing your greenhouses. But, you could not tell who had the biggest plants just by observing them.

Measuring gave you a way to compare your plants to your teammates' plants.

> I was right. One of my plants is taller than all of your plants!

Measuring gives you more data so you can describe your plants more accurately. Describing things as accurately as possible is important in science. It lets you compare your observations to the observations of others.

Evidence

Look at the picture to the right.

What do you think has happened to the apple? Why do you think so?

Compare your My Amazing Beans Record Page from Lesson 1 to the Are They Growing? Record Page that you made today.

Have your beans changed? Why do you think so?

The observations that you recorded are **evidence** that your beans have changed.

Evidence is information that helps you know something.

Finding evidence is an important part of scientific investigations. Scientists explain things by using evidence to show how they know something.

What evidence do you have to show which plants have grown the most?

Checking Understanding

1. Talk about these questions with your teammates.

   What is evidence?

   What have you done to collect evidence during the greenhouse investigation? Use your record pages to help you.

2. On your own, write your answers to the questions.

3. Put the paper in your own science folder when you are finished.

How Could You Find Out

You collected evidence to show which plants have grown the most.

- How could you find out how much one plant grows in a week?

Investigating Plants' Needs

Your class transplanted the bean plants and made a list that shows what you think the plants will need in order to keep growing.

How could you find out if plants really do need these things to live and grow?

C.Q. and I.O. Plan an Investigation

Find out if plants need the things on your list to live and grow.

How will you set up your investigation?

We are going to help you plan an investigation to find out if your plants need some of the things on your list.

Investigating is fun, if you know what to do. We have some ideas to get you started.

If you want to know if plants need water, you can find out what happens when plants do not get water. You can do this by . . .

What if you want to know if plants need light? You can find out what happens when plants do not get light. You can do this by . . .

What about air?
You can find out what happens when plants do not get air. You can do this by . . .

Finish this sentence, too!

Talk about your ideas with your classmates. Decide on the best way to find out if plants need water, light, and air.

Investigating the Needs of Plants

Your class decided on the best way to find out if plants need water, light, and air. You made charts showing how you would do each investigation. Set up the investigations. Watch closely and find out what happens.

Set up your investigations.
Collect evidence that shows if plants need the things on your list to live.

Team Skill

Share and take turns.

Team Jobs

Manager

Tracker

Messenger

Team Supplies

all teammates' plants

the class Investigation Charts

petroleum jelly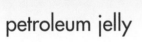

Directions for Investigating the Needs of Plants

Share supplies and take turns doing the tasks.

1. As a team, decide which investigation each of you will set up.

2. Do these things on your own.

   ▶ Follow the directions and set up the investigation.

   ▶ Share with your teammates what you did to set up your investigation.

3. Do these things as a team.

   ▶ Set your investigation plants where you can observe them every day.

   ▶ Pick 3 of your team's plants that are not part of the investigations. These plants will be your **compare to** plants.

      ▶ Write the word "water" on a label.

      ▶ Put the water label on one plant.

      ▶ Put that plant next to the plant that gets no water so that you can compare them.

Water

No Water

► Write the word "light" on a label.

   ► Put the light label on another plant.

Can you put the plants with the labels "light" and "no light" in the same place? Why or why not?

► Write the word "air" on a label.

   ► Put the air label on the third plant.

   ► Put that plant next to the one that gets no air so you can compare them.

You want the soil to be moist but not too wet.

4. Water all of your **compare to** plants by doing these things.

▶ Check the plants every day. If the soil feels dry, add one medicine cup of water.

▶ Wait until the water soaks in and test the soil again.

▶ If it still feels dry, add a second medicine cup of water.

On Your Own

Making Observations and Keeping Records

Observe your team's **investigation** plants and **compare to** plants every day.

Use the top part of the Investigation Record Page to record your observations of the **investigation** plants.

Today my **investigation** plant(s) looked like this.

Use the bottom of the Investigation Record Page to record your observations of the **compare to** plants.

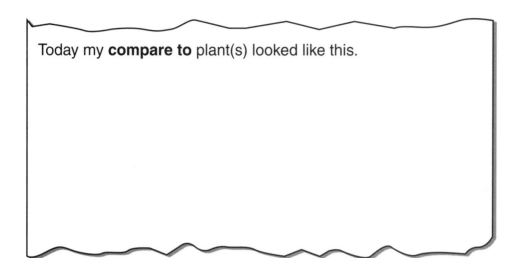

Today my **compare to** plant(s) looked like this.

Compare your observations of the **investigation** plants to your observations of the **compare to** plants.

▶ Do the **investigation** plants look different from the **compare to** plants? Why do you think so?

▶ How are they the same? How are they different? Draw pictures and write about your plants.

▶ Keep your records in your science folder.

Compare your observations to your teammates' observations.

Are your observations always the same as your teammates' observations? Why or why not?

Checking Understanding

1. Talk about this question with your teammates.

   ▶ Why do you think the **compare to** plants are part of the investigations?

   ▶ Write a team answer that you can share with the class.

2. Predict what you think your investigations will show.

   Write or draw your predictions.

How Could You Find Out

 What other things are on your list of plants' needs? What could you do to find out if your plants need these things too?

Plant Part Chart

Describe the different parts you have seen on your bean plants.

What do you think these parts do for the plants?

Why do you think so?

Share your ideas with the class before you go on.

Plants are made up of many different parts or **structures**. The structures work together to help a plant get what it needs to live and grow.

You have seen some plant parts at work as you observed your growing bean plants.

Roots

As your bean plants first started to grow, **roots** appeared from the seeds. The roots grew down to the water in the bottom of your greenhouse.

Roots have long, thin root hairs that soak up water. Some roots can store water until other parts of the plant need it.

Roots also soak up or **absorb** nutrients. Nutrients are the minerals that plants need. Plants cannot live without nutrients.

Nutrients are often found in the soil where plants are growing. The potting soil you buy at the store has nutrients in it. Sometimes people grow plants in water—without soil! The nutrients for these plants are added to the water.

Roots do another kind of work for plants. They hold the plants tightly in the ground. Could you feel how tightly the bean plants' roots held on when you tried to remove them from your plastic bag greenhouse?

Soon after the roots appeared from your bean seeds, another new plant structure showed up!

Stems

For a while, it might have looked like your bean seeds were growing long, skinny necks. These neck-like things are **stems**.

Stems connect a plant's roots to its leaves. Water travels from the roots, through the stem, to other parts of the plant. As the plant gets bigger, the stem gets bigger and stronger.

Leaves

The last things to appear on your bean plant were the **leaves**. Your bean seeds opened and the first leaves came out.

The two halves of the bean seed looked like leaves for a while, but they dropped off as the plant grew bigger.

The leaves help your plants get air and light. Plants use air and light to make their food.

Air enters through small openings on the leaves. If air cannot get through these openings, the leaf will die.

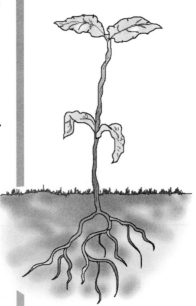

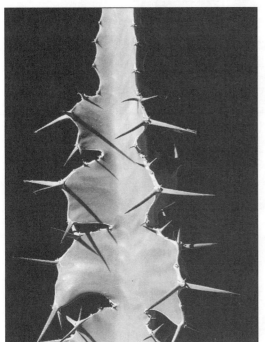

Not all leaves use air and water to make food for the plant. The prickly spines on a cactus plant are leaves, but they do not make food. A cactus makes food in its green stem.

Not all leaves look like the leaves on your bean plants. The needles on a pine tree are leaves, but they look and feel very different from bean plant leaves.

Flowers

After plants, like your bean plants, have grown enough, they produce **flowers**. Flowers do very important work. They produce the plants' seeds.

Fruit

Some flowering plants, like beans, package their seeds inside **fruit**. Fruits develop from parts of the flower. The seeds are inside of fruit such as apples, green peppers, nuts, and bean pods!

Seeds

Some plants, like your bean plants, begin as **seeds**. You might have seen an **embryo**, or young plant, when you observed the insides of beans in Lesson 2.

The soft material in the middle of the bean is the **cotyledon**. The growing embryo uses the cotyledon for food.

Food gives the energy that all living things need to live and grow. Both plants and people need energy. Plants do not eat food for energy like we do. Plants have parts that use energy from sunlight to make food. Then plants use the food for energy to live and grow. Plant embryos use the cotyledon for energy. Some bigger plants have leaves where the energy is made from air, water, and sunlight.

The **seed coat** is the outside of the bean. When dry, the seed coat is very hard.

Some plants produce seeds but not flowers. Pine trees produce their seeds in pine cones. 📖

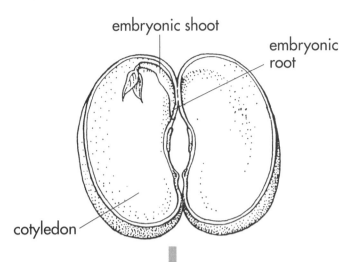

embryonic shoot

embryonic root

cotyledon

Taking a Second Look at the Plant Part Chart

By reading, you have gathered evidence about what plant structures do.

Compare this evidence to your ideas on the Plant Part Chart.

Are there any changes you want to make to the chart?

Team Task
List any changes you would make to the Plant Part Chart. List your evidence for making the changes.

Team Skill

Share and take turns.

Team Jobs

Manager   Tracker   Messenger

Team Supplies

paper

pencils

Directions for Taking a Second Look at the Plant Part Chart

Take turns talking and sharing ideas.

1. Compare the information on the Plant Part Chart to the information you just read.

   Talk with your teammates about new ideas you have.

2. Decide with your teammates if the class should change anything on the Plant Part Chart.

   ▶ If so, what should be changed?

   ▶ Why do you think it should be changed?

3. On the paper, write the changes you would make to the Plant Part Chart.

4. Write your evidence.

   Be ready to share your changes and evidence with the class.

Checking Understanding

1. As a team, share your changes and evidence with the class.

   ▶ Be ready to answer questions from other teams.

   ▶ Be ready to give evidence to support your changes.

2. On your own, listen to the other teams' changes.

   ▶ Decide if you agree with their changes.

   ▶ Be ready to tell if you agree or disagree, and why.

How Could You Find Out

Other kinds of plants may have parts that are different from parts of your bean plants. The parts might do different things than the bean plant parts do.

- How could you find out about some plants that have different parts?
- How could you find out what those parts do?

Needs and Structures

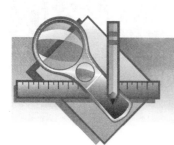

On Your Own

Sharing Your Observations

Share your observations of your investigations.
Find out what your classmates are observing.
Do these things to tell your classmates about your investigations.

Put your paper in your science folder when you are finished.

▶ Write and draw about what is happening in your investigations.

▶ Write a sentence that tells if you think plants need water, light, and air.

▶ Draw a picture that shows why you think so.

▶ Use your record pages as evidence for your ideas.

Making a Needs and Parts Poster

Observing your investigations and reading are two ways that you found out about the parts of plants. You now know that those structures help plants to meet their needs.

Show what you have found out. Make a poster that matches the parts of plants to the needs they help meet.

Team Task
Make a Needs and Parts Poster

Team Skill

Students do their jobs.

Team Jobs

Manager   Tracker   Messenger

Team Supplies

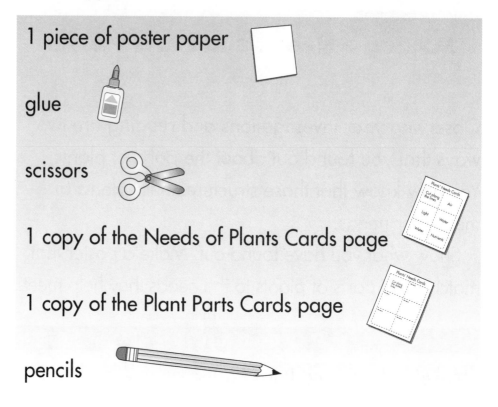

1 piece of poster paper

glue

scissors

1 copy of the Needs of Plants Cards page

1 copy of the Plant Parts Cards page

pencils

Directions for Making a Needs and Parts Poster

1. Make a poster that looks like this.

Needs and Parts Poster	
Needs of Plants	Plant Parts

2. Cut out the Needs and Parts Cards.

▶ Put the Needs Cards in one pile.

▶ Put the Parts Cards in another pile.

3. Lay the Needs and Parts Cards out in front of you.

4. Decide as a team how to match each Needs Card with a Parts Card. Do these things to help you decide.

▶ Pick one Needs Card.

▶ Talk about which part helps the plant to meet this need.

▶ Find that part on a Parts Card.

▶ Put the two cards side by side.

▶ Do all teammates agree with this match?

▶ If not, discuss the other Parts Cards until you all agree.

▶ If you do agree with the match, glue the Needs and Parts Cards to your poster.

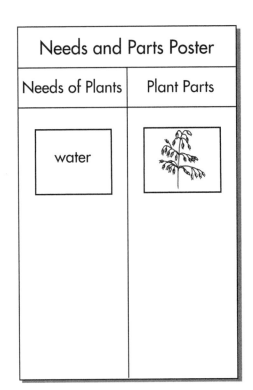

Needs and Parts Poster	
Needs of Plants	Plant Parts
water	

5. Repeat Step 4 for each of the Needs Cards.

6. After you have matched all the Needs and Parts Cards, hang your poster on the wall.

Comparing the Needs and Parts Posters

Do you think all the posters will be alike? Observe and find out!

Team Task
Compare your team's poster with those of other teams. Talk about how they are alike or different. Write how they are different.

Team Skill

Do your job.

Team Jobs

Manager

Tracker

Messenger

Team Supplies

1 sheet of writing paper

1 pencil

Directions for Comparing Needs and Parts Posters

1. Decide who will write first.
2. Look at other teams' posters.
   ▶ Talk about how they are like your poster.
   ▶ Talk about how they are different from your poster.
3. Write how the posters are different from yours.
4. Be ready to discuss the differences with the class.

Checking Understanding

1. Write one new idea you have about what plants need and how they get what they need.
   Share the evidence that shows how you know.
2. Put your paper in your science folder.

Plant Patrol

You are learning a lot about plants! By observing your investigations, you are learning what plants need to live and grow. By reading Plant Parts at Work, you found out about the structures that help plants meet their needs.

You have learned all this by observing and studying the bean plants in your classroom. What about the plants outside? How do they meet their needs and survive?

Observing Outdoor Plants

Observe the plants in your school yard or a nearby park. Find evidence that shows how the plants get what they need to live and grow.

Team Task

Observe different kinds of plants out-of-doors.
Record your observations by drawing pictures.
Compare your drawings.

Team Skill

Share and take turns.

Team Jobs

Manager   Tracker   Messenger

Team Supplies

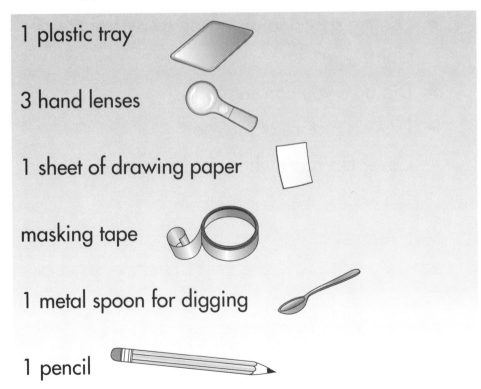

1 plastic tray

3 hand lenses

1 sheet of drawing paper

masking tape

1 metal spoon for digging

1 pencil

▶ Do not taste any of the plants.

▶ Ask your teacher for permission before touching any plants. Some plants might not be safe for you to touch.

Directions for Observing Outdoor Plants

1. Tape the sheet of paper to your tray.

2. Observe as many different kinds of plants as you can find.

3. Record your observations by doing these things.

    ▶ Draw pictures of the plants you observe.

    ▶ Label the parts of the plants.

4. Observe the roots of the plants by doing these things.

    ▶ Use the spoon to move soil away from the plant.

    ▶ Dig until you can see roots.

    ▶ Draw a picture of the roots.

    ▶ Cover the roots when you are done.

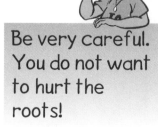

Be very careful. You do not want to hurt the roots!

5. Compare your pictures of the plants. Talk about these things with your teammates.

▶ How are the plants alike?

▶ How are the plants different?

▶ How do you think they get what they need to live and grow?

Write your ideas on your paper.

6. Be ready to share your pictures and ideas for a class chart.

George Washington Carver
(1864-1943)

The farmers gathered around George's horse-drawn wagon.

They had a problem and they needed help. The cotton plants were not growing well and an insect, the boll weevil, was killing the few cotton plants that did grow.

"Why not grow peanuts instead?" George quietly asked the farmers.

The farmers were surprised. They were cotton farmers, not peanut farmers! They grew cotton because the cotton fibers, found inside the flower of that plant, were used to make yarn and cloth. But, why grow peanuts? Other than hog food, what could peanuts be used for?

The farmers thought that George might be crazy! But, they knew that the African-American scientist was very smart. He had helped them before and had taught them many things about growing plants. They knew he was a very kind man who loved plants and everything in nature. So, the farmers listened carefully to George.

George explained to the farmers that peanut plants would grow easily in this environment. He said that the plants needed only sunshine, some rainfall, and sandy soil to grow and be healthy. George explained that peanut plants would give the worn-out Alabama soil a rest so that the farmers could plant cotton later. He told them that the boll weevil would not bother the peanut plants.

"Just plant them," George smiled as he told the farmers, "and I'll find ways to use the peanuts."

So, the farmers went to work planting peanuts and George went to work in his lab. He did not have a fancy lab—just a room filled with bottles, old kitchen utensils, and odd containers. He worked night and day making foods and other things from the fruit of the plant—the peanut. George loved his work so much and worked so hard that his students had to remind him to eat and sleep. He made salad oil, ice cream, peanut milk, instant coffee, vinegar, and, best of all, **peanut butter**! But, he didn't stop there. He made over 300 different things from peanuts!

It had not been easy to convince the farmers to plant peanuts. Making changes is not easy. But, challenges like this one were not new to George. He faced many in his lifetime. George learned a lot about peanut plants by investigating. He knew that peanut plants could get what they needed to survive and grow in this environment. Because he learned so much about the needs of peanut plants, George Washington Carver was able to help the farmers and give us peanut butter, too!

Sharing
IDEAS

Exploring More Outdoor Plants

These plants grow in very different places.

Write your answers to the questions. Be ready to share your ideas with the class.

1. Do you think the plants in the pictures can meet their need for air, light, and water? Why do you think so?

2. What might make it hard for plants to meet their needs in these places?

3. How are the parts of these plants different? How are they alike?

4. How do you think the parts help the plants get what they need in these places?

Checking Understanding

Use your imagination to show how plant parts help meet the needs of plants. Be creative!

1. Do these things on your own.

   ▶ Draw a picture of a make-believe plant from Mars.

   ▶ Make a list of the things that this plant needs to live and grow. You know that plants on earth need air, light, and water. But, you can make up the things that the plant from Mars needs.

▶ Show all the structures that help the plant from Mars get what it needs to live and grow.

▶ Write how the parts work to help the plant live and grow.

How Could You Find Out

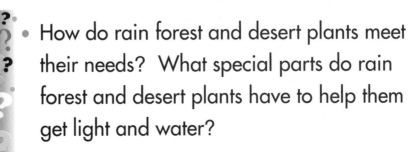

• How do rain forest and desert plants meet their needs? What special parts do rain forest and desert plants have to help them get light and water?

• Find out by getting books and magazines from your school's library. Read about rain forest plants and desert plants.

My Plant Book

Scientists often write books that show what they have found out from investigations.

Make a book that shows what you have found out about the needs of plants.

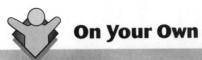
On Your Own

Making a Book About the Needs of Plants

Your Task
Make a book about the needs of plants.

Your Supplies

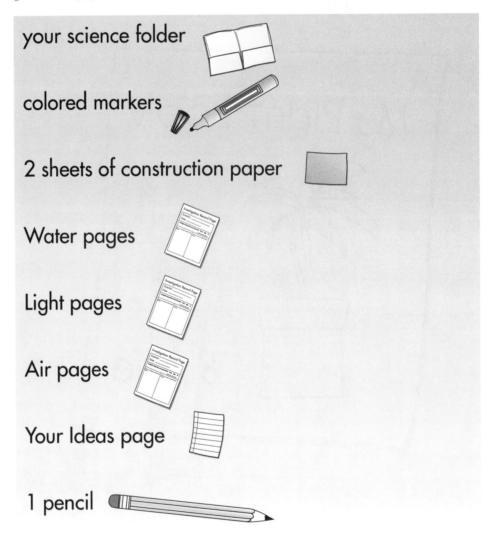

your science folder

colored markers

2 sheets of construction paper

Water pages

Light pages

Air pages

Your Ideas page

1 pencil

Directions for Making a Book About the Needs of Plants

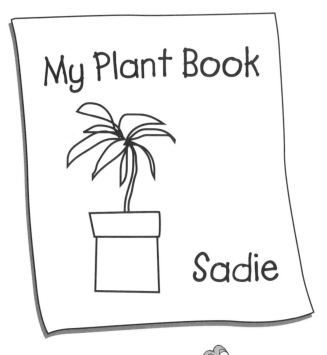

1. Make a front and back cover for your book.

   ▶ Decorate the covers using your colored markers.

   ▶ Write your name on the bottom of the front cover.

2. Sort your record pages to prepare your evidence.

   ▶ Put your water observations in one pile.

   ▶ Put your light observations in another pile.

   ▶ Put your air observations in a third pile.

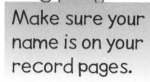
Make sure your name is on your record pages.

3. Follow the directions on the book pages for water, light, and air.

4. Staple your book together.

Sharing
IDEAS

Share the interesting or exciting ideas you wrote about on the Your Ideas page. Find out what your classmates found interesting.

What else would you like to know about plants?

Acknowledgments

Photo Credits

Carlye Calvin, pp. 2–13, except as indicated below;
  p. 43, p. 59 middle, p. 60 bottom

National Center for Atmospheric Research,
  p. 2 center right, p. 4 bottom, p. 6 bottom,
  p. 7 bottom

William J. Weber/Visuals Unlimited, p. 56

Brian P. Foss/Visuals Unlimited, p. 59 bottom

E. Webber/Visuals Unlimited, p. 60 top

Corbis-Bettmann Archive, p. 80

John D. Cunningham/Visuals Unlimited, p. 82 top

Joe McDonald/Visuals Unlimited, p. 82 bottom

Special thanks to the administration, teachers, students, and parents of John Adams Elementary School, Colorado Springs, Colorado, for allowing us to photograph students "doing science." pp. 1–18

Art Credits

Linn Trochim; *BSCS Biology: An Ecological Approach;*
  BSCS art files.

Design and Prepress

PC&F, Inc., Hudson, New Hampshire

Cover

Leaves courtesy of Corel
Plant image © 1996 PhotoDisc